TO:

FROM:

Praise for EMPOWERED PRODUCTIVITY

"Based on what you taught us, and in the days following your training, I was able to get my inbox down from nearly two hundred to zero messages and create a master task list to guide my days. I am thrilled and feel a huge sense of relief. Using Empowered Productivity, I have been able to keep my inbox at zero messages for several days and feel confident that the progress will continue into the future. I'm so grateful that my leadership team invested in Empowered Productivity training!"

—*Dawn Palma, Chief Administrative Officer, U.S. Army Corps of Engineers, Hydrologic Engineering Center*

"I wanted to thank you for [teaching us Empowered Productivity]. In all honesty, I was a little bit of a pessimist at the beginning, but since have "bit"—hook, line, and sinker. Since...my implementation of your system, I feel like a weight has been lifted off my shoulders that I hadn't realized was there. Your system has changed my life. I feel so much more productive and organized, which in turn gives me a great feeling of accomplishment at the end of the day. Thank you so much for your help! I am a true believer!"

—*Connor Fox, Product Specialist, Medtronic*

"My sixty-four pages of inbox messages is now empty... I have been processing incoming email for a week... My sweetheart wonders if I am the same person! [Empowered Productivity] has been life-changing information for me. Thank you again."

—*Linda Lindquist, Owner, Protect Your PCs*

"[Empowered Productivity] made the whole staff cognizant of how we use email, and the quantity of staff email dropped off considerably right away. So, thanks again for this important and relevant work you're doing. It's changed everything at work (and some things at home!)."

—*Debi Vanwey, Finance Director, Sustainable Food Center*

"I did find [Empowered Productivity] extremely valuable, and it has absolutely changed the way I work. I am more organized, and I am accomplishing a lot more day in and day out for myself, my team, and the organization as a whole. I've made meetings more impactful, I've managed my emails better, I have been able to more effectively work through multiple projects simultaneously, and I still get normal day-to-day activities done. Thanks again!"

—*Sue Godfrey, Senior Manager, CUNA Mutual Group*

THE

HAPPY INBOX

HOW TO HAVE A
STRESS-FREE RELATIONSHIP WITH
YOUR EMAIL AND OVERCOME
YOUR COMMUNICATION CLUTTER

MAURA NEVEL THOMAS

simple truths
▶ Small books. BIG IMPACT.

IGNITE READS
spark impact in just one hour

Internal images © endpapers, page iii, iStock/Getty Images; page vi, nesharm/Getty Images; pages x, 97, Maskot/Getty Images; page xiv, JGalione/Getty Images; page 7, massimo colombo/Getty Images; page 15, sturti/Getty Images; page 20, Sviatlana Yankouskaya/EyeEm/Getty Images; page 26, nortonrsx/Getty Images; page 32, Willie B. Thomas/Getty Images; page 38, Carina König/EyeEm/Getty Images; page 43, Kosamtu/Getty Images; page 48, Prostock-Studio/Getty Images; pages 54, 70, 102, Westend61/Getty Images; page 62, jacoblund/Getty Images; page 79, Delmaine Donson/Getty Images; page 84, FreshSplash/Getty Images; page 88, Fiordaliso/Getty Images; page 109, Drazen Zigic/Getty Images; page 112, visualspace/Getty Images; page 116, Constantine Johnny/Getty Images; page 122, DjordjeDjurdjevic/Getty Images

Published by Simple Truths, an imprint of Sourcebooks
P.O. Box 4410, Naperville, Illinois 60567-4410
(630) 961-3900

Printed and bound in China.
OGP 10 9 8 7 6 5 4 3 2 1

I am so grateful to my mother for her decision to move us close to family when I was a baby. That move gave me a rock-solid group of people who have been such an important constant in my life. This book is dedicated to those childhood neighbors who have become lifetime friends and extended family: Kerrin and the McGillicuddys, Shannon and the Murphys, Dennis and the O'Neills, and also Karen, Kelly, Joyce, Marianne, and Laura. Thank you for being my "village." I love you all.

TABLE OF

CONTENTS

THE EMPOWERED PRODUCTIVITY SERIES

My first book, *Personal Productivity Secrets* (Wiley, 2012), was the first published work detailing my **Empowered Productivity System**, which I had been delivering to clients for many years.

Since then, the world of work has continued to evolve. It has left the confines of the office. I write this now in quarantine because of the global COVID-19 pandemic. "Knowledge workers" are required to be more creative and innovative than ever before. But they have less and less time and space to marshal their mental resources in a thoughtful way because of the countless and increasing demands on their attention.

In the decade since I wrote that book, I've been honored to work with some of the world's most influential leaders and brands. That experience has both refined my thinking and given me the opportunity to defend it in some of the country's most prestigious business outlets. The result is the latest evolution of the Empowered Productivity System, which has been put through much more rigorous testing and refining, incorporating input and feedback now from more than forty thousand professionals.

This book, detailing the Communication Management portion of the System, is the third in the Empowered Productivity Series from Ignite Reads, after *Attention Management: How to Create Success and Gain Productivity—Every Day*, published in 2019, and *From To-Do to Done: How to Go from Busy to Productive by Mastering Your To-Do List*, published in June of 2021.

I'm confident that the latest version of my Empowered Productivity System, as presented in this series, is the best it's ever been. I'm excited and humbled to join you on your journey to peak productivity and to help empower **your** ability to achieve the results that are most significant to you, personally and professionally. I look forward to seeing the results as more and more people like you can bring your unique gifts to the world in a way that inspires, motivates, and excites you rather than exhausts, overwhelms, and stresses you.

INTRODUCTION

MANAGING COMMUNICATION AND INFORMATION

Our biggest productivity hurdle today might just be our communication—our crazy inboxes, our constant phone notifications. In the modern workplace, we must navigate the "always on" pings from technology that distract us and entrap us in a constant state of task switching. You know how this feels: You're trying to work on something, but then there's an email to answer. Then a text message. And oh, look: a social media notification!

Spending your days reacting to these distractions isn't just unproductive. It also means you aren't in the driver's seat of your own life. Constant reaction means relinquishing control rather than being intentional.

In this Communication Management component of the Empowered Productivity System, you'll learn more about how to conquer the distractions caused by information and communication overload and how to get out from under "communication debt" so you can live a life of choice—one of action, not reaction.

The concept of communication debt seems to have been coined by tech entrepreneur Henry Poydar. To paraphrase, it's that state of feeling like you always owe return communication to someone. It's the subtle sense of anxiety caused by your backlog of communication, taunting you with the little red indicators on the communication apps on your phone—texts, voicemails, missed calls, social media notifications—plus the mountain of outstanding email piling up in your inbox even as you read this.

This book will also help you enjoy the other benefits that come from managing communication and information effectively:

▸ You'll reduce anxiety caused by digital and paper clutter.

▸ You'll minimize the amount of communication you send and receive.

▸ You'll be able to retrieve information you need quickly.

▸ You'll collaborate more effectively.

The first step in managing communication is to tackle your inbox. The strategies that follow will help you destress, declutter, and regain control over your email!

ONE

GETTING YOUR EMAIL UNDER CONTROL

We're starting with email for a reason. It attacks our productivity on a variety of fronts:

- ▸ Too many email messages are unimportant, which makes those that *are* important difficult to recognize.

- ▸ Those unimportant messages steal time that you could be spending on proactive, focused work.

- ▸ The constant stream of incoming emails distracts you and causes you to get stuck in reactive mode.

- ▸ A full inbox weighs on you and creates stress.

- ▸ Email frequently contains tasks you must accomplish, so when you aren't in control of your email, you aren't in control of your workload.

- ▸ Bad email habits impede collaboration and create inefficiency among colleagues, weighing down organizations.

It's important to note that there's no magic bullet for managing email. No app or feature or trick is going to instantly get your inbox under control. But there are four specific reasons that people get buried under a mountain of email, and Empowered Productivity offers a solution for each one. If you follow the steps outlined in this book, you'll soon be relieved of the stress that an inbox (or inboxes!) with hundreds, thousands, or tens of thousands of messages is causing you.

Your Inbox Is for Receiving Messages, Not Storing Them

Part of the problem with the stress of email is that we're so used to it, we are often convinced that it isn't there. It's hard to recognize the magnitude of the stress we're under until we're not under it anymore. I often speak with people in my engagements who say, "Yes, I have thousands of messages in my email inbox, but who cares? I know what's been dealt with." This means they are using their inbox for storage. But your inbox is not for storing messages; it's for receiving and processing messages.

Let's consider for a minute your physical mailbox at your home or office. I know that a lot of snail mail isn't important anymore, but if you're old enough to remember when everything important came in the mail, or if you can imagine the world before electronic communication, when everything was delivered as physical mail, let's do a little exercise.

Picture the physical mailbox at your house or office. Imagine that every day, you got the mail, opened it, looked at it, and then put it all back in the mailbox. Tomorrow, your letter carrier comes and puts that day's mail on top of the mail you've already looked at. Then imagine this process happens day after day after day. (Yes, you'll have to imagine your mailbox is much bigger than it actually is.) You've looked at all the mail, you've noted the bills that need to be paid and the other correspondence that needs attention, but it's all piled in with everything else, including a lot of junk mail. Maybe you throw some of that away, but there are some catalogs and fliers that you think you might want to check out sometime, so those are in the pile too.

After a month or two of all your new mail being piled on top of your opened mail and things you might want to look at someday, are you really sure you're on top of everything that needed attention? Wouldn't you be a little concerned that you might have missed something important? Doesn't the pile just get more daunting (and more cluttered) with each passing day?

It's not a perfect analogy, but that's mostly what it's like when you use your email inbox to store messages you've already looked at. I'm not saying you shouldn't save whatever messages you want to save. I'm just saying you shouldn't store things that you've already read **in your inbox**. Here's the way most people deal with their email in my experience:

1. Read every message as it comes in, or as soon as you can.

2. If it's definitely junk, delete it.

3. If it doesn't require a reply, leave it in your inbox and move on to the next message.

4. If it needs just a quick reply, send that, leave the

message in your inbox, and move on to the next message.

5 If it needs a more lengthy reply or maybe contains other tasks you need to complete before you can reply, mark it as unread or flag it so you know you need to deal with it later.

I call this behavior "skim and skip." Now I have three questions for you, and you need to be honest with yourself when you consider your answers:

1 Do those five steps above mostly describe how you deal with your email?

2 When you see it in black and white, does it really seem efficient to you?

3 How many times do you read the same message over again?

There is a better way, and the first step is recognizing that storing all messages in your inbox—read, unread, not requiring action, maybe requiring action, and definitely requiring action—is a big part of the problem.

Instead, start thinking about your email inbox as the place where incoming messages land, and your goal for your inbox is to read those messages, make a decision about them, and move them out of your inbox as quickly as you can. This doesn't mean you have to complete all the required actions that every email demands. It just means you have to capture the necessary actions in the correct place (usually your task manager—check out the prior book in this series, *From To-Do to Done*, for more on this) and then move the email **out of your inbox** to an appropriate storage location.

You Don't Filter

The second reason that most people find themselves buried in email is because we all get more than we could ever read, so for greater efficiency, we need to filter the messages in a way that makes them more manageable.

Chances are your inbox holds a wide assortment of email, from spam to newsletters to discount offers to important communications from your boss or colleagues. With all these different and varied messages vying for your attention, it's overwhelming to sort everything out and take appropriate action.

The second step of communication management in the Empowered Productivity System is to make smarter use of email filters. The email we receive can fall into one of four categories:

1 Spam

2 Unwanted "robomail" (mass messages sent via an email marketing service)

3 Wanted robomail

4 Work (real messages from individual people addressed specifically to you)

The following is advice for automated handling of each type to save you time and effort.

1. SPAM

I'm sure you have an idea what spam is, but let's define it in the context of Empowered Productivity. Spam is malicious messages from unscrupulous companies that don't follow laws and norms of ethical marketing. They try to trick you into giving out sensitive information, add malware or spyware to your computer, infect your computer with a virus, or use other malicious or underhanded tactics. Sometimes we lump other kinds of messages into the category of spam, but in this context, I mean messages that truly aren't legitimate and that you never want to receive.

Email hosting providers, software, apps, and cybersecurity features are getting better and better at preventing these messages from ending up in your inbox, so you may never see them. If you do, you should report them to your company IT department or your email hosting provider. If you're ever suspicious about a message, even if it seems to come from someone you know, don't click any links! Reach out to that person via a different medium and confirm they sent it.

2. UNWANTED ROBOMAIL

Robomail is a term used to describe automated marketing messages. They are mass mailings sent via email marketing services that are usually triggered by an action you've taken, such as making a purchase, taking advantage of an offer, or requesting information or support assistance. Sometimes people you meet at business functions will also add you to their newsletter list without asking, which is rude, but usually not malicious. Many people offhandedly refer to messages in this category as spam, but they aren't. You can tell the difference because a legitimate marketing message from a reputable company will have an unsubscribe link somewhere in the message. Technically, reputable companies shouldn't send you marketing messages without your permission, but the definition of permission is applied broadly.

I'm sure you get plenty of these messages that you don't want and you don't read. These messages fall into the unwanted robomail category. There are a variety of techniques you can use to automatically prevent these messages from ending up in your email inbox:

▸ Click the unsubscribe link in the message. These are usually handled by a third-party email marketing service that will automatically prevent future messages from that company being sent to you.

▸ Use an unsubscribe service. These are increasingly popular and can work well. You can do an internet search for the term and find a comparison page to evaluate them or post on social media to ask your friends and contacts what services they use. You'll probably have some tech-savvy friends who have tried many and can make a good recommendation for you.

▶ Create a rule in your email application so any messages coming from that specific email address or that domain (@xyzcompany) will automatically be diverted to your Trash folder.

For information on unsubscribe services I use and recommend, and instructions on creating rules in the most popular email applications, visit *maurathomas .com/control-your-tech.*

You might find that just one or some combination of these techniques is necessary. For a while, it will take an extra few seconds per message to deal with unwanted robomail, but after a few days or a week, the number of messages you receive in this category should drastically decrease, providing a big return on that time investment.

3. WANTED ROBOMAIL

These are similar to the prior category, but the difference is that you actually want these messages. They could be newsletters you enjoy reading, advertisements from the companies you frequently do business with, or newsletters from groups you belong to. Some of these you read regularly, and some of them you read only infrequently, but you wouldn't mind receiving them if they didn't distract you. The Empowered Productivity technique for handling these types of messages is to divert them from your primary inbox to a place where you can review them at your convenience. Many of the unsubscribe services mentioned earlier provide this kind of repository (like a web page, an app for your device, or both) and will send you one digest message daily, with a link to each message. You can scroll through the digest and/or open the app or web page when you want to review the messages individually.

You can also create rules for these types of

messages so they get diverted into a newsletter or similarly named folder so you can peruse them at your convenience. But I really like the digest feature of some services.

These suggestions are useful for lists you're already on with your primary email address. Another necessary step is to prevent future robomail from landing in your primary email inbox. One way to do this is by having a free, secondary account that you use to subscribe to things, such as when you make what you expect to be a one-time purchase or when you need to provide your email address in exchange for information you would like to receive. You can scroll through that secondary account at your leisure to see if there is anything that interests you.

A second way to prevent future robomail from landing in your primary inbox is to use a service that creates a dynamic email address through a browser plugin. If you visit a page that asks for your email address in exchange for something you want, the plugin will offer you the opportunity to create one of these dynamic email addresses instead of providing your primary email address. All messages sent to that dynamic email address go to one repository location as I described earlier, and you can opt to receive one daily digest with a summary of all the messages received. Unsubscribe services also offer the opportunity to block access in the future if you decide never to receive those messages again, so unsubscribing isn't necessary. These services, daily digests, and block-access options provide an advantage over the free, secondary address I described above.

For example, you may have noticed that it's very common for books like this one to offer supplemental information on a website (such as the links I've included throughout this book), which is sometimes only available by providing your email address. Authors do this for several reasons. First, we believe that if you are interested enough to read our book, you are likely to be interested in other information from us, and we'd like to be able to connect with our readers. Second, it helps us to keep the books shorter and more concise. If you want supplemental information, it's available to you, but the main information in the book can be faster and easier to consume. Lastly, it helps to keep the information current. The publishing world moves slowly, and recommending services in a book that may not be published for a year or more can make parts of the book outdated before it even ends up in your hands. This way, we can keep the information fresh and relevant.

Depending on the book and how relevant you feel the information is, by employing the techniques discussed, you can opt to receive the messages at your primary email address so you can read them soon after they arrive, or you can also receive them at your secondary email address or repository for your new email management service, either of which you can review at your convenience. I receive some of my most relevant but routine communications via these dynamic email address services.

4. WORK

The last category of email is individual messages from real people, addressed specifically to you. These are messages from coworkers, clients, prospects, vendors, friends, and colleagues. They are messages that you need or want to read, so I put these in the category of work. The goal with the email filtering technique of Empowered Productivity is that the only messages that reach your primary inbox are messages that fall into this category. This filtering technique automatically prevents you from having to sift through thousands of messages and try to prioritize what needs your attention the soonest. By employing the tactics described earlier, you'll minimize the number of messages that arrive in your primary inbox every day, and you'll know that whatever arrives there will need your attention sooner rather than later. Personally, I have reduced the volume of email I receive by over **70 percent** by employing a combination of these techniques!

You Have the Wrong Perspective on Email

The third reason people get buried in their email is because, in my experience, a lot of professionals seem to believe they should be able to squeeze in managing email around their "real work." They view it as an extra activity they need to do in addition to their work.

But the fact is, email in the last category above *is* real work, and you must treat it like real work that takes real time. Those messages from your boss, your colleagues, your customers, and your vendors merit your focused attention, not just a quick glance and a dashed-off reply between meetings.

Once you've shifted your thinking to recognize these types of emails as real work, you then have to allow that it takes real time to address these messages in a thoughtful way so you can make a favorable impression on colleagues, supervisors, clients, prospects, and others in your professional and personal networks, and keep your commitments to them.

There have been many predictions about the demise of email, and while studies show the volume has dropped a bit in the last decade, it's been holding steady recently. I expect email communication to be something we'll continue to use professionally for a long time.

After appropriate filtering, the professionals I work with receive about one hundred emails a day, and this is in line with email surveys at the time of this writing. If we figure that on average, each of those emails takes about two minutes to process, then we're looking at almost three and a half hours a day just to manage email.

Now consider that these same professionals typically also have several hours of meetings each day, and you can see why there's a problem if you'd like to work only eight or nine hours in a day. Over three hours of email every day, plus three or more hours of meetings per day, leaves very little time to get any other work done! If this describes you, you aren't just drowning in email you don't have time to address. This email overload is also hampering your ability to get anything else done! The overflow work is probably seeping into your personal life, causing you to check email at the dinner table, at your child's school functions, late into the night, and during vacations, because it seems like constant checking is the only way to stay on top of it. But this robs you of the time you need to rest and rejuvenate.

Consider this a wake-up call. If this describes you, you're headed for burnout. And it's important that you get real about your schedule and everything that's on your plate.

Your Email Is Full of Actions You Need to Take

You probably didn't realize it at the time, but all the work you put into setting up your calendar and your task list using the Action Management component of the Empowered Productivity System (detailed in the prior book in this series, *From To-Do to Done*) will now help you manage your email.

Here's why. The last reason most people's email inbox gets overwhelming is because they use it as a task list. But if you've read *From To-Do to Done*, you know more about how to manage your actions, and you might recognize at least two reasons why using your email as a task list isn't helpful. First, not everything you have to do comes to you via email, so if you have some of your tasks (from your thoughts, meetings, and other communication channels) in your task manager, and some of your tasks in your email inbox, it's like trying to do a puzzle when half the pieces are in the dining room and half the pieces are in the kitchen. You don't have a good handle on everything that's on your plate, and you can't allocate your attention appropriately.

Also, if you leave a message in your inbox that is really one or more tasks you have to complete, you can't know without reading the email again (and again and again) exactly what needs to be done, by when, and how you should prioritize it given everything else you're working on.

But if you implement the Empowered Productivity System, including for managing your actions, you can escape this trap. Instead of checking your email repeatedly to stay on top of your work, you can move tasks or commitments out of your inbox and into your task manager. This ensures you are on top of everything you need to do, allows you to organize and prioritize appropriately, and gives you the peace of mind of knowing that nothing will fall through the cracks.

TWO

BEING REACTIVE VS. BEING RESPONSIVE

The prospect of handling your email differently might make you feel a little anxious. "I'd like to have more control and feel less overwhelmed," you may be thinking. "But my job requires me to be responsive. Is it really possible to do both?"

Absolutely! But there's an important distinction to make here. You *do* have a responsibility to respond to the many daily emails and other communications you receive in a timely manner. Of course, the definition of "timely" varies according to the specific message, and it's something you need to determine for yourself. But it's probably longer than you assume. I've worked with companies whose employees felt that delivering anything less than an immediate response meant they weren't providing good customer service. However, email is *not* a synchronous communication tool, meaning a real-time, back-and-forth dialogue, such as when you are having a conversation. Therefore, it's inefficient to treat it as one. In most industries, checking email periodically throughout the day is sufficient.

Email is in fact asynchronous, intended to have a built-in time delay of minutes, hours, or even days between communications. You *do not* have an obligation to constantly and immediately act on every piece of communication you receive. If you try, you'll never get anything important done. You'll also be training yourself to become bored in the absence of that constant stimulation. Focus and concentration are like any other skill: if you don't use them, you lose them.

The Empowered Productivity techniques for staying on top of your email ensure that you can be thoughtfully responsive and also keep email from dominating your days.

The Things You *Shouldn't* Do with Email

The tactics below might make you feel like you're doing something to get your email under control, but they're actually counterproductive.

► Marking emails that require action as unread or with a flag so that you'll come back to them later. It's not efficient to read the same email more than once.

► Assigning categories to the messages in your inbox.

► Leaving your email inbox open and visible so that each new message calls your attention away from whatever else you were doing.

The problem with these practices is that they make it necessary to check multiple places (your task list and your inbox) to get the full picture of everything that's on your plate. Setting boundaries around your email enables you to have more productive days. Rather than checking your email constantly and stopping what you're doing to immediately react to every message, a better approach is to "batch" your email management. Choose times in your day when you give your email inbox your focused attention for an extended period of time so you can process your messages. Processing means dealing appropriately with every message so you can move it out of your inbox by deleting it, filing it, or adding the appropriate action or actions to your task list. However, depending on the nature of your job, you might need to review your inbox in between processing times.

Reviewing Email: Dealing with the Quick Stuff

If you're used to constantly checking your email all day long, it's going to be hard to break that habit. And only you can decide how often you should check your messages. If people are used to receiving an immediate response from you, it's going to be tempting to continue. But just like you taught others to expect an immediate response by always giving them one, now you can teach them that it will take you a little longer to respond. They can learn this over time by your behavior, or you could consider putting a line in your email signature that reads something like, "I only check email periodically throughout the day. If your message is of a more urgent or timely nature, please call me."

"Reviewing" your email, in the context of Empowered Productivity, means skimming your messages quickly to identify which ones are urgent and need a quick reply, which ones can be immediately deleted or quickly filed, and which ones can be resolved with a quick action like

a phone call. This review is to eliminate all the fast and easy messages and ensure there is nothing urgent.

How Often to Review

How often you should review your email is up to you, but it's probably less often than you think. The important thing to remember is to scan your email **in between** other tasks, not **during** other tasks. When you're doing something else, resist the urge to switch to check your email. Close your inbox to remove the temptation. Finish the task you were working on, and then check your messages if you think you should.

The nature of your job can help you determine how often you should review your email. If your job is very reactive, such as support roles (customer service, IT, human resources), then you may need to review your messages hourly. If you have a more independent role, like in leadership, or a very detail-oriented role, like in finance or programming, you should probably review your messages less often. For many professionals, reviewing messages two or three times per day is plenty.

The timing of your email reviews also depends on your job. If it works for you, it's great to give yourself proactive time at the start of the day by working from your task list first thing in the morning and waiting to review messages until midmorning. But it may work better in your situation to review your messages first thing in the morning to look for information that directly affects your plans for the day. (Do this review from your phone or other portable device if you can, instead of your computer. That will make it harder for you to let email derail your plans for the day, since it's more difficult to manage messages on your phone's small keyboard.)

Here are a few more questions to consider as you think about whether reviewing email in the morning is right for you:

▸ **Are you an independent professional (self-employed) or a remote worker, or do you work in an office with other people?** If you work with others, you're less likely to miss something important if you decide not to review your email in the morning and go straight to your task list. That's because someone will likely pop in to tell you about what's going on, or you'll overhear something. But if you work independently or remotely, an email review may be more necessary in the morning.

▸ **Do you have time to be proactive, or do you have to rush off to a meeting?** The whole point of not reviewing email first thing in the morning is to be proactive and work from your task list. If you need to rush off to a meeting, you don't have time to be proactive anyway, so go ahead and review. Besides, reviewing your email will alert you if the meeting has been delayed or canceled.

▸ **Do you work with people in another time zone?** If you work closely with people who are getting ready to leave work around the same time that you are arriving, then it makes sense to review your messages in case you need to deal with anything before the close of their business day. In this case, set a timer to remind you to move away from email and work from your task list. This will prevent you from spending too much time in your email and staying in "reactive mode" all day.

▸ **What expectations have you set with others around email?** It's easier to skip a morning email review if others don't expect immediate replies when they email you. See page 31 for more about how to reset expectations about email.

Don't Get Stuck in Review Mode

Reviewing should be part of how you handle email, but it can't be the only thing you do. If you never go back and act on those messages that require time or thought, they are soon lost in a black hole of hundreds or thousands of messages.

You still don't really know how important those messages are, how to prioritize them within the rest of your workload, what specific actions they might require of you, or how much time those actions will take you. Deferred emails nag at you and cause anxiety. You know you need to do something with them, but you don't know what that is. And you constantly worry that you're missing something important.

As those ill-defined tasks pile up in your inbox, it becomes difficult or impossible to figure out how much work is really on your plate now or where the tasks lurking in your email fit in with your other priorities. It also becomes more and more likely that something will fall through the cracks.

THREE

PROCESSING EMAIL: "DONE FOR NOW"

The next part of your email management is processing. Processing doesn't require that you complete all the tasks associated with your email messages, only that you deal with each message to the point that it is not hanging around as an unknown that causes you stress. When you process your email, you make the decisions needed to get each message out of your inbox.

Here are the steps to follow when you set aside

those times during your day to process your email.* If you're wondering how often you need to process your email, start with around three hours per day, based on the one hundred messages at two minutes per message estimate discussed on page 22. Maybe that's one hour, three times per day, or maybe it's divided up into other intervals. But know that if you don't leave any time to deal with your email today, you're going to have six hours or more to answer tomorrow, so plan appropriately. I often have two-day stretches during my week where I get on a plane, travel to a client, deliver a client speaking or training engagement, and then fly back home. I have very little time to answer emails during these two-day periods, so I

---

*   As I explain this part of the Communication Management component of the Empowered Productivity System, I'm describing it as if you can get your inbox empty on the very first day. I understand that you may have hundreds, thousands, or tens of thousands of messages in your inbox right now. When I explain how to get started, I'll tell you how to deal with that. As you read the next sections, assume you have at most only a few days' worth of messages in your inbox.

leave the third day that week as unscheduled as I can. That gives me the opportunity to tackle the six hours of messages I fell behind on while traveling, plus the additional three hours of messages that will arrive on that third day. I don't empty my inbox every day, but I do empty it at least once every week or so. Otherwise, I live with the unsettling feeling that I'm missing important things.* The amount of time you need to manage email will decrease as you work through the filtering steps discussed in chapter 1.

When you've reached that point in your day when it's time to process your messages, first, set your email to offline mode so new messages stop arriving. Otherwise, by the time you finish addressing one message, another one (or two or more) will have arrived. You'll never make it past the most immediate messages. Think about managing email like digging a

---

* For more on how I catch up when I get behind, read: https://
maurathomas.com/productivity/overwhelmed-tips-to-regain
-control-over-your-work-and-life/.

hole. If your goal is to empty your inbox (get to the bottom of the hole), every new message that comes in is like someone standing beside you, throwing the dirt back in every time you shovel it out! For instructions on how to set most popular email applications to offline mode, visit *maurathomas.com/control-your-tech*.

After setting your email to offline mode, you'll next want to sort your emails in a variety of ways to help you quickly identify what's there and act upon them in the most efficient ways. First, organize your messages by subject (or thread) if they aren't already. This ensures you don't spend time on an issue that was already handled. Next, sort by sender to quickly delete or file anything unimportant or "FYI" that you didn't catch in your prior reviews. Then work through your messages in whatever order makes the most sense for you. Some people stay in the sender sort and jump around based on the most important senders. Some people start with the oldest first, because those senders have been waiting the longest for a reply. Others find it most

efficient to read the newest messages first. The specific order at this point doesn't really matter, because the goal is to get to all of them anyway.

Commit to reading each message fully, however long it takes. Resist the urge to skim a message and skip over it. This is just procrastination; you're going to have to deal with the message eventually, so it might as well be now.

Before moving on to the next message, do whatever is required to move that message out of your inbox. To help you make these decisions faster, I created the TESST process. Here's an overview:

- **T**ake immediate action.
- **E**mpower others and yourself (delegate).
- **S**uspend it to your task list to take the required action later.
- **S**tore it for future reference.
- **T**rash it.

Now let's take a closer look at each step of the process.

PUT IT TO THE TESST

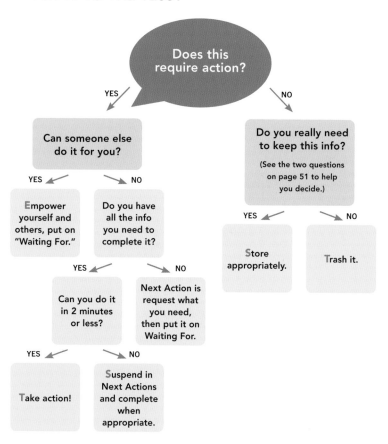

1. Take Immediate Action

For each message you need to process, first ask yourself, "Does this require action? Is there anything I need to do, either now or in the future, related to this email?" If an email can be resolved with a task that takes you two minutes or less (like writing a brief reply), go ahead and do that task. Then you can either delete or file the email.

2. Empower Others and Yourself

Some emails require action, but that doesn't necessarily mean you are the best person to perform that action. In those cases, it's best to empower someone else to take action. For example, let's say you receive an email request from someone outside the organization that requires a response. You could respond yourself, but you have a team member who can also respond and who needs to build experience with this type of request. By asking your team member to handle the request, you are empowering their professional development. Forward the message, or if it requires a detailed explanation, create a Next Action from the email to request a meeting or phone call to explain the task. And if you need to follow up on any of the tasks you delegate, add a Waiting For item to your task list.

Delegating to team members, family members, or people you hire via outsourcing services also empowers you. It frees you up to do the things that you do best, the things that only you can do, and the things that have the biggest impact on your work and your life. For example, if you don't spend as much time with your kids as you would like and your Saturdays are often taken up by yard work, you might hire a landscaping service. This empowers you to do the things that are more important to you and empowers a local business owner to gain a new client.

If you're in sales and you feel that too much time is absorbed with travel planning and other administration, you might hire an hourly virtual assistant for a few

hours a week. This kind of delegation again empowers both you and a small business owner or freelancer.

3. Suspend It to Your Next Actions

This is an important one. Some emails will require actions, and you'll be the best person to take those actions (in other words, they're not good candidates for delegating). But the actions will take more than two minutes to complete. These tasks might just be more time-consuming, or perhaps you need more information or someone else's help to complete them. Instead of pausing your processing time to deal with these actions, **enter them in your task manager to act on later.**

Don't just leave a message in your inbox, thinking it will serve as a reminder to complete a task. Remember, to be productive, you need to have only *one* central place to look for all the things you need to do. When you see an email that requires action but you leave it in your inbox, you're essentially creating a second task list. That leads to stress and inefficiency. Add the task to your main list. For instructions on how to turn an email into a task using common email and task management apps, visit *maurathomas.com/tools*.

4. Store It for Future Reference

If an email doesn't require action, or if you've already completed the required action or added it to your task list, the next step is figuring out whether you should save the message or delete it.

If you're like many professionals I've worked with, you tend to keep more emails than you really need to. Depending on how much storage space you have and how well the search feature in your email application works, this might not matter. Or you may work in an industry where you need to save every message for legal reasons. But if you save them, *don't* save them in your inbox.

If you aren't sure whether you need to save them, asking yourself two simple questions will help you choose and clean up the clutter of messages you'll probably never look at again. When deciding whether to hit delete or save the email (in a different email folder), ask yourself:

1. **Could you easily get the information in the email from another source if it turns out you do need it later?** For example, is the information on your company's intranet? Could a coworker or other department at your company provide it? Could you just search the web for it? If you can find the information again without too much effort, then you don't need to keep the email.

2. **What's the worst thing that would happen if you later thought you needed this email but didn't have it?** When I ask my clients this question, the answer is often a shrug of their shoulders. If you can't even think of a consequence for not keeping the email, or the worst consequence might be a minor inconvenience, then you can safely discard it.

To organize the emails you save, you don't need some elaborate system of folders and subfolders. When you have a lot of folders, it takes longer to decide where to file a particular email and more time to find it when you need it.

Keep the number of folders you use to a minimum. If you receive both business and personal email at the same address, create a folder for each of those categories. Then you might want one more level of categorization within your folder for business email (internal, clients, project-related, etc.).

Instead of relying on a folder system to help you retrieve filed emails, make use of the search and sort features in your email client, which are quite powerful. In addition to searching for words or phrases, you usually have the capability to sort by date, sender, subject, and a host of other options. With these features and just a few folders, you should be able to find any email in a matter of seconds. Just remember, your inbox is for **receiving** messages, not **storing** messages.

5. Trash It

Delete any emails that no longer require action and that you don't need to save for reference. Personally, I hit the Delete button on emails often. But I have my email client (Apple Mail) set so that emails are never automatically deleted from the Trash folder. That way, if it turns out that I need it later, it's never really gone. If I run low on storage, I eventually mass delete the oldest messages from the Trash folder.

Now you're done! By successfully processing your email, you've set yourself up for more productivity and less stress. You'll get better and better at processing the more you do it. Eventually, you might need only about three or four hours twice per week to effectively process your messages through your system. Using an organized process is worth every minute you spend, in terms of both productivity and the control and peace of mind you get in return.

FOUR

IF YOU NEED A FRESH START

———

You have now learned everything you need to control your email moving forward. But I know that you might currently be buried in messages. If you have thousands or tens of thousands of messages in your inbox right now, it's not a good use of your time to try to go through and selectively file them. But that backlog can prevent you from starting fresh.

You might have heard of people declaring "email bankruptcy"—simply deleting all of their email messages and starting over, or just abandoning their current email address and creating a new one. I have an alternate plan for you that's less drastic, but still helps you escape that sense of overload and get some momentum for moving forward.

1   First, prevent new messages from arriving. Your email client will determine how you do this, such as by switching to offline mode (most clients), pausing your inbox (Gmail), or changing your preference from "download new messages automatically" to "download new messages manually" (Apple Mail).

2   Next, create a folder named something like "Old Emails," or if you really think the majority of messages in your inbox are still relevant and you need to go through them, name the folder "Old Email to Process." Move everything before yesterday or the last few days into that folder. How far back you go is up to you. The point is to leave

only a manageable number of the most recent messages in your inbox that you can process right away. If you're pressed for time, maybe leave twenty to thirty messages. If you have a little more time, maybe leave as many as fifty. Everything else will still be in that other folder when you need it, but this will enable you to start fresh with your new process.

3 Resist the temptation to pick and choose the messages you leave in your inbox. This will take too much time and won't provide a return. Just leave the messages that are the most recent, and move everything else. Moving forward, your goal will be to move each message *out* of your inbox once you've read it.

4 Process the messages that are left in your inbox using the TESST process until your inbox is empty.

5 You can work through the Old Email to Process

folder when you have some time, or wait until something comes up (like someone saying, "Did you get the email I sent you last week?").

How to Get Less Email

Now that you have the opportunity to start fresh in your inbox, you should know about some additional ways to make your email easier to manage going forward. One way to do that is to reduce the number of messages that get to you in the first place. You have more control over this than you might think! You learned several techniques in chapter 1, the four reasons you're drowning in email, and steps you can take to change that. Following are ways you can influence *others* to perhaps send *you* fewer messages.

TAKE SOME CONVERSATIONS OFF EMAIL

In the early days of email, we had to use it for just about everything because we didn't have many other alternatives. Today, that's changed. Now we have an array of communication tools, and some of them handle certain tasks a lot better than email does. For example, online schedulers can help you eliminate all the back-and-forth emails when you are trying to set up a meeting with people who are not on your shared calendar.

If you are going back and forth with someone more than about three times, you might ask them when they can take five minutes to jump on the phone with you and conclude the issue that way. If your topic is sensitive or complex, email is usually not the best medium. Face-to-face conversations or video calls are better options.

CHANGE OTHERS' EXPECTATIONS

Getting less email isn't just about making smarter use of technology. It's also about the expectations you create with others about how you will use email.

Do you make it a point to respond to all emails as quickly as you can? That sends a message to others that they can immediately get their questions answered or problems solved if they email you. People do what gets results, and if they get quick results by emailing you, they're going to keep doing that.

It's up to you to reset their expectations. This doesn't mean that you start ignoring emails. It just means that you start getting people used to the idea that they will receive a response from you within, say, three hours instead of instantaneously. At first, you might get some pushback on this. People might text or drop by your desk to ask, "Hey, didn't you get my email?" But that's fine. Once they get used to your new response window, they'll adjust. And perhaps they'll even start searching out answers on their own instead of defaulting to emailing you!

ADOPT EMAIL BEST PRACTICES

There's one more important thing you can do to reduce the number of emails you have to manage: put more thought into the emails you send. This helps cut down on miscommunications and on endless back-and-forth exchanges that don't accomplish anything. At the same time, you'll be helping your colleagues reduce the amount of email they have to deal with, making them more productive as well.

Composing more effective emails isn't hard, either. Start considering these questions whenever you begin to compose a message. They'll soon become second nature.

Is email the best way to communicate this?

Sometimes the most productive email is the one you end up not sending. Email tends to be our default form of communication, but it's not always the best way to communicate.

Would it be easier to handle this on a phone call?

Email *seems* faster than a phone call, and some people prefer to avoid the human contact. But that "one quick message" often leads to a long thread, wasting your

time and your colleagues' time. Often, a phone call provides quicker resolution.

Are you being super careful with your phrasing?

This is a signal that you're dealing with a sensitive topic that's best discussed in a conversation instead of email. Emails are more likely to be misunderstood because the recipient doesn't have as many clues (like your demeanor or tone of voice) to help them interpret what you really mean.

Are you sending this email to the right people?

Sometimes we copy extra people unnecessarily because we aren't sure of the right recipient. But this just wastes others' time. Make your best guess, but then ask them, "If you aren't the right person to receive this message, could you let me know who is?"

Do you really need to "reply all"?

For the sake of overburdened email inboxes everywhere, think twice before you send an email encouraging a "reply all" or respond to one with a "reply all." It's probably the fastest option for you in the moment, but ultimately, it's not the most efficient way to collect group feedback. When I work with large companies, I often see huge labor and talent costs because people send group messages using "reply all," instantly creating dozens of messages for their colleagues to deal with. If someone is collecting input, respond only to them, and then let them report on everyone's feedback. If you have a message for just one recipient, don't send it to everyone with "reply all."

Do you really need to cc other people?

Overusing email ccs creates more work for your colleagues, sows confusion, and sets the stage for "reply all" emails. Whenever you start to copy someone else on a message, stop to consider whether the cc is really needed. You might think it's polite to keep everyone in the loop (and it's certainly low effort), but in reality, we end up burying our colleagues in messages and information.

A cc often fails to get across the information you intend to convey. First, the people copied have to read the message to determine whether it's even relevant to them. Second, they may not glean from it what you want them to know. Third, unless a message is addressed to them, recipients of a cc may not even read it. This confusion is one of the top causes of communication breakdowns.

If you want to inform someone about part of a message you have sent to someone else, cut and paste the information from the first message into a separate email that you send directly to the person. Because you're telling them exactly what you want them to know, there is no chance for misinterpretation, and less of a chance that your coworker will overlook the message.

Another option is to address the cc'd coworker directly in the original message, near the top. For example, "Hi, Shannon. I'm writing to summarize our meeting. Marianne, I'm copying you because I wanted you to know what we agreed upon yesterday."

Another common reason for cc'ing others on an email is a practice politely abbreviated as CYA (which less politely stands for cover your a**). For example, if you aren't sure the plan you're suggesting in an email is the best course of action, you copy your boss on the message, figuring she'll correct you if she doesn't agree. But she probably never reads the message, and the fact that you copied her does not absolve you of responsibility anyway.

A better plan is to run your intentions by your boss prior to the communication. Or you can include your boss in the "to" line, address her directly in the message, and invite her input. For example, "Karen, I think we should go with the 5×7 flier. Joyce, please let me know if you disagree."

Do you really need to bcc other people?

There *is* a good use for bcc: when you are emailing many people, using bcc keeps recipients from seeing one another's email addresses, *and* it also keeps them from replying all! But outside that use, there's a lot of potential for harm when you bcc to share a message with someone when you don't want the actual recipient to know. Ethics aside, you've probably heard (or experienced) at least one unfortunate situation of a bcc gone embarrassingly awry, with someone sharing sensitive information publicly because they didn't realize they were bcc'd.

Instead of using bcc, it's better to go into your Sent folder and forward the message to the other recipient, explaining why they are receiving it: "Laura, below is the message I sent to Dennis to call attention to his frequent tardiness."

What should the subject line be?

Can you convey your whole message (or at least the most useful part of it) with the subject line? Remember that your recipients are very likely to be reading your email on their mobile devices, where space is limited and opening and closing messages requires extra taps that waste time. When possible, write your subject lines in such a way that someone who's checking their messages on their mobile device doesn't have to open your email to get the key information.

To show you what I mean, let's consider this sample email.

SUBJECT: Important information regarding today's meeting!

BODY: The meeting has been canceled.

Revising this email to put the relevant information (the meeting has been canceled) in the subject line would have been more effective and more courteous to the recipients. Even if you needed to convey additional details in the body of the email ("We'll reschedule next week when John is back in town."), your recipients would still get the essential information they need without having to open the message.

Even when you can't fit all the essential information into the subject line, you'll still help others if you are as descriptive and specific as possible, especially if you are asking the recipients to do something. "Please review agenda before Fri. meeting" or even "ACTION REQUIRED re: Friday meeting" are more helpful subject lines than "Friday meeting."

Don't jump the thread.

The phrase *jump the thread* means replying to a message about one topic with a response about a second topic without changing the subject line. For example:

INITIAL MESSAGE SUBJECT: Action steps from the meeting

INITIAL MESSAGE BODY: We agreed in the meeting that the following people would take the following actions…

RESPONSE MESSAGE SUBJECT: RE: Action steps from the meeting

RESPONSE MESSAGE BODY: Thank you. I also wanted to let you know that I spoke with the customer regarding that issue we discussed last week…

This responder has jumped the thread, bringing up an issue totally unrelated to the one indicated by the subject line of the initial message. It is very easy to overlook or automatically delete messages like this, especially if the recipient assumes that the original issue is resolved. Instead, start a new message with an appropriate subject line. Some people use the old thread with a new subject line, but a new message is a lot cleaner than a set of old messages that can confuse the recipient with unrelated information in a message history.

What needs to be in the body of the email?

Like the subject line, the body of your email should be short, descriptive, and specific. Get to your point quickly. In our fast-paced, short-attention-span, time-starved environment, brevity is welcome. Sometimes background information is helpful, but understand that most readers choose to read a short email over a long one, saving a long message to review later—but often later never comes.

Don't assume that the recipient knows the action

(if any) you want them to take after reading the email. You'll save them time if you spell it out. For example:

The meeting is scheduled for noon Friday. **Please let me know if you can join us.**

Here are the finalists for the new logo. **Please respond with your three favorites by tomorrow.**

Here's a copy of Debra's report. **No action needed.** But you might find her conclusions on page four relevant to your work with the client.

What would move the conversation forward?

Have you ever been on an email thread like this?

YOU: Hey, we need to get together. Are you free Tuesday at 1 or Wednesday at 3?

RECIPIENT: No, sorry.

YOU: How about Thursday at 9 or Friday at 2?

RECIPIENT: No, those don't work for me either.

Annoying, right? And it's causing both you and the recipient to send a bunch of unnecessary emails and waste a lot of time. To head off exchanges like this one, make sure that any email you send moves the conversation forward.

To move the conversation forward, your recipient should have answered your first email with a reply like this:

No, sorry. But I can do Wednesday at 1:30 if that works for you.

But you also could have anticipated the potential communications roadblock and made your initial message more like this one:

Hey, we need to get together. Are you free

Tuesday at 1 or Wednesday at 3? If those are bad, please propose some times next week that work for you.

When you anticipate roadblocks, you become a more efficient email communicator, and that saves time for both you and the recipients of your emails.

Does this email need a numbered list?

Have you ever noticed that when you send someone an email with several topics, they answer maybe the first one or two and ignore the rest? There are a couple of ways around that. First, you can make it a habit to cover just a single topic in each email, but that results in more messages, so it isn't always more efficient. Instead, I have another tip for getting all your points addressed that's almost magical.

Instead of using paragraphs or bullets, **number your points**. Yes, it's that simple. Our brains really respond to numbers. If, for example, your email has three numbered points, the recipient will feel like they haven't completed the email until they address all three. It gives your recipients that feel-good sensation of checking items off a list.

Numbers also make it easier for your recipient to respond because it gives them a shorthand. They can just reply quickly with something like:

1 Yes.

2 No.

3 I'll get back to you on that.

In every aspect of your job, you have a responsibility for clear communication that enhances productivity. Email is no different. Writing more productive emails enables you to set an example for communication within your organization, minimize communication breakdowns, reduce email clutter, and save everyone some time.

Managing Other Communication Channels

You can apply what you just learned about email to the other methods of communication you use as well. As with email, the key thing to remember about managing any other communication channel is that it should serve you, not the other way around. Remember that the measure of your productivity is how much progress you have made on the results that are significant to you—*not* how quickly you respond to the latest notification.

As you did with email, put some limits around how your other communication channels push information to you, and make sure you're moving tasks to your task list. You don't need the stress of worrying that you're overlooking work hidden in your text messages, voicemails, or other communication channels. Below are some of my recommendations, by channel, to better manage all the communication that comes your way.

PHONE

If you're old enough, you remember the days when a phone was used just to make and receive calls. (Hey, it wasn't *that* long ago!) Now your phone can be a vehicle for countless other communication channels, including several kinds of text and instant messages, direct messages, emails, and yes, even the occasional phone call. Colleagues, family, and friends use your phone to get your attention, but so do the games and other apps you downloaded, as well as all the marketers who have your contact information.

If you read the first book in this series, *Attention Management: How to Create Success and Gain Productivity—Every Day*, you know that constantly keeping one eye on your phone makes it all but impossible to accomplish meaningful work or have meaningful interactions with others. And you understand how your phone also feeds a habit of distraction. If you haven't already started setting your phone to Do Not Disturb or silent sometimes, especially when you're

trying to focus on another activity, start experimenting with how that feels now. This is also a good time to switch off notifications from games, news sites, and other apps. You can learn about "persuasive technology" and how these apps are manipulating you in *Attention Management*.

TEXT MESSAGES

These are becoming increasingly popular for work communication. Texts can be useful in some situations, such as for people who spend their days on the go as opposed to at a desk. One of the challenges text messages pose is that they imply an immediate response is required. Sending a text can make it seem like whatever is being communicated is an emergency, and recipients often feel compelled to respond, even when the issue isn't urgent. And if you can't or choose not to respond in the moment, it's easy for text messages to get forgotten or lost because they can't be marked, tracked, or organized like email messages can. This often makes texts a poor tool for business communication, except in the case of truly urgent or time-sensitive issues.

Your job might require you to be away from a desk or an office most of the day, making email communication inconvenient (because your phone is too small to effectively manage your email and your laptop is too large to lug around with you). In that case I suggest using a tablet, so you can keep your work communication out of your texting app.

Texts for business communication also pose a challenge to work–life balance, because when business contacts have your personal cell number, not everyone is respectful about business hours, and it's hard to get away from business when you're not working. If you routinely use your personal cell phone for business but would also like to create more boundaries around your personal time, try a virtual phone number that you can silence or forward when necessary. As of this writing, the most common of these is Google Voice, but there are others. Learn more at *maurathomas.com/ control-your-tech.*

SOCIAL MEDIA

Giving any advice about social media is tricky business. There are always new networks, and the specific rules of each network always seem to be changing. Social media also play different roles in the lives of different people. Your social media channels might be part of your job, or they might be a distraction from your work. Or you might pay little attention to them at all!

Because of all those variables, there's no one way to define using social media productively. But I can give you a few overall pointers that should stand the test of time no matter the changes to the social media landscape.

▸ Unless your social media channels are a critical part of your job responsibilities, turn off notifications from them.

▸ Realize that checking your social media channels as a break from work isn't much of a break at all if your work involves looking at screens. The break has to be a different type of activity *to your brain*. Switching from reading spreadsheets while working to reading sports scores or your friends' social media updates won't provide a break for your brain. It's more restorative to do a quick meditation, take a quick catnap, or move your body—preferably in the outdoors.

▸ If you start noticing that your time on social media sites seems to be keeping you from making progress on things that are important to you, consider scaling back your use, taking a social media break, or making it less convenient to get on these sites, such as by removing the apps from your phone or not storing your passwords, so you have to type your login information every time.

▸ You should also pay attention to how you *feel* after using social media. If your social media time leaves you feeling happy, inspired, and connected to others, that's great. But if you're feeling anger, jealousy, a sense of inferiority, or other negative emotions, that's another good reason to consider a social media break.

TEAM COMMUNICATION TOOLS

Many companies are introducing team communication tools into their organizations, sometimes in an effort to make information more accessible and sometimes to cut down on emails. But most companies make the mistake of not providing any guidelines as to which communication tool should be used in which situation. The result is that instead of making team communication more efficient, it doubles or triples the amount of communication created.

Another major problem of these is that they magnify the "got a minute?" drop-ins of your physical work space via their instant messaging feature. This means that you not only get interrupted by those in the same physical space with you, but any colleague anywhere in the world can "drop in" on you. I've worked with many clients to address the distraction problems that these team communication tools create inside companies.

One way to make team communication tools more efficient is to agree with your team on how you will use each channel that is available to you. You can never plan for every eventuality, so these shouldn't be considered rules, just guidelines. The following chart is an example to get you started.

Type of Communication	During Business Hours	Outside Business Hours
Email	Routine requests, information sharing	Hold or use delay send
Team communication tools (Slack, Teams, etc.)	Project related communication, socializing	Everyone set to Do Not Disturb
Phone, video calls	Relationship-building, sensitive or complex topics	Time-sensitive or urgent only
Text	Time-sensitive or urgent only	Time-sensitive or urgent only

For more on my favorite team communication tool, how to be more efficient with your communication channels, and a downloadable version of the preceding chart that you can edit for your own team, visit *maurathomas.com/tools.*

FIVE

MEETING MANAGEMENT

When you think about drains on your productivity, meetings are probably right up there with email. My clients and the staff at my client companies often complain that they spend too much time in meetings—about three to five hours per day on average—with dubious results.

But just as with email, you don't have to passively accept all the meetings that end up on your calendar (especially if they are put there by others). There are ways you can exert more control over the meetings in your schedule. When you do that by following the suggestions in this chapter, you'll help make meetings more productive for yourself and for your colleagues, and you'll improve the meeting culture at your organization. You'll also free up more time for everyone to spend on the activities that require more of your "brainpower momentum," and make the biggest difference for your role and your organization's success.

Before the Meeting: Productive Planning

If you're the organizer of a meeting, you can take steps right from the outset to make sure the meeting produces the results you are looking for while still being respectful of others' time (and your own!).

SET MEETING GOALS

If you're the meeting planner, get clear about its purpose. Fill in this blank: "At the end of the meeting we will have/know/do _____." A meeting is most useful when it will advance an agenda, so you must be very clear about the decision or decisions that you expect to be made in the meeting. Share this goal and these decisions when you invite people to your meeting.

If you are invited to a meeting and the ultimate goals and decisions expected to come out of the meeting are not clear, that's a red flag that the meeting may be less productive than it could be. You'll do everyone a favor by asking the meeting planner to provide that information and share it with the attendees.

Some meetings are simply to provide updates, with a secondary goal of getting everyone together for interaction, discussion, camaraderie, and collaboration. Examples include meetings of a board of directors, special interest group, or volunteer group. This type of agenda is useful in this setting, but inside organizations, the benefit of this interaction must be considered in relation to the number of meetings everyone is invited to daily. For example, if the team at your company is bogged down by hours of meetings every day, meetings with this type of goal should be evaluated carefully. A more effective option might be to build socializing time into other meetings, and provide project updates via your team collaboration tool.

DECIDE IF THE MEETING IS REALLY NECESSARY

The next question to consider as the meeting planner: Does this meeting need to happen at all? The way to determine this is to ask yourself, "Given how busy everyone is, do the benefits of accomplishing this goal via face-to-face, synchronous communication outweigh the time the meeting attendees will have to give up for it?"

If, for example, you're trying to collect input on a document, there are other ways to accomplish that without having a meeting. You could put the document in a shared file that others can then review and comment on at their convenience, asynchronously, any time before a deadline that you provide. Another example is if you're trying to collect opinions, in which case you could create a quick online survey with free survey tools.

SET THE AGENDA

Every meeting should have an agenda, a start time, *and* an end time. Go one step further on your agenda by assigning time limits, or at least guidelines, for each topic on the agenda. When you do this, you'll be able to see whether your desired agenda fits into the time allotted for the meeting. If your agenda doesn't require an hour, by all means schedule a shorter meeting. The attendees will thank you! If you try to jam ninety minutes or more of agenda items into a one-hour meeting, that's also going to be a problem.

An agenda with time limits empowers everyone in the room to keep the meeting on track, without hurting anyone's feelings. If someone is going on and on in a meeting or if you realize the conversation isn't productive, you can point back to the agenda and say something like, "This is a really interesting discussion, but according to the agenda, we're running behind. These other topics are important, so let's make a decision or table this discussion for a later date." Or if the discussion turns out to be unexpectedly important, you can make the decision, individually or as a group, to reschedule some or all of the other agenda items so you can continue the discussion.

CHOOSE THE RIGHT TIME OF DAY

Decision fatigue is the idea that our ability to make rational decisions is eroded throughout a day of making decisions, because the act of making decisions runs down our mental energy.* Decisions can range from whether we should hit the gas or the brake when

---

* John Tierney, "Do You Suffer from Decision Fatigue?" *New York Times*, August 17, 2011, https://www.nytimes.com/2011/08/21/magazine/do-you-suffer-from-decision-fatigue.html.

we see a yellow light, to which employee to hire, to whether to accept a job offer. Small or large, each decision makes a withdrawal from our bank of mental energy. The scientific term for decision fatigue is *ego depletion*. This concept was originally put forward by Roy Baumeister in the late 1990s, based on a well-known chocolate chip cookie study he conducted.[*] Recently, there has been some debate in the scientific community about whether ego depletion is real; this question was raised because the results of that study couldn't be replicated, casting doubt on the study's conclusions. Further study was deemed inconclusive.[**]

I will leave it to the psychologists to debate from a scientific perspective, but I know that decision fatigue

---

[*] Hans Villarica, "The Chocolate-and-Radish Experiment That Birthed the Modern Conception of Willpower," *The Atlantic*, April 9, 2012, https://www.theatlantic.com/health/archive/2012/04/the-chocolate-and-radish-experiment-that-birthed-the-modern-conception-of-willpower/255544.

[**] Malte Friese et al., "Is Ego Depletion Real? An Analysis of Arguments," *Personality and Social Psychology Review* 23, no. 2 (May 2019): 107–31, https://doi.org/10.1177/1088868318762183.

is real for me. Judge for yourself. Have you ever come home from a long day at work and had someone ask you to make a decision, even one as simple as what you want to have for dinner, and your response was "I don't care"? And you responded this way because you just couldn't bear the thought of making one more decision that day? If you've had this experience, my suggestion is that decision fatigue is real for you too.

If we accept the premise of decision fatigue, that would suggest that meetings to make important decisions should not be scheduled for the end of the day or other times when people are low on energy, such as right before lunch (many people skip breakfast and are very hungry and therefore lacking energy at this time) or right after lunch (many people get drowsy and hit that midafternoon slump after lunch). So that leaves us with the mornings for these types of meetings. If it's common in your organization for your team to be checking their email first thing in the morning, then that's a good time to schedule a meeting

where important decisions need to be made (although I suggest that you encourage them to adopt the more productive habit of working from their task list first thing). If most people in your organization seem to use first thing in the morning for their "deep work" (which is more productive), then schedule meetings requiring important decisions for midmorning, such as 10:00 a.m. or thereabouts. For more on how to empower your team to do their best work, check out my earlier work, *Work Without Walls: An Executive's Guide to Attention Management, Productivity, and the Future of Work.*

HONOR THE CLOCK

A meeting planner should always honor the clock— start on time and end on time! A common problem I see in companies is that they never start meetings on time, because people are always late. This is a problem that propagates itself: if there are people who are habitually late to a meeting, others will start to come late too, because they know that sitting in a room waiting for a meeting to start isn't a good use of their time. Before long, no one will be on time, and this will create a culture of unproductive meetings where no one can plan their days effectively, because none of their meetings start or end on time. As the organizer of meetings like this, you'll get a reputation in your company as someone who doesn't run meetings well, and then people will be less likely to show up to your meetings. If key leaders are the biggest offenders of arriving late to meetings, devise ways of accounting for this. Here are some suggestions:

1. Start your meetings at quarter after the hour. This might provide some breathing room between meetings for attendees to use the restroom, grab a beverage or a snack, and make it from one meeting room to another in time.

2. Instead of scheduling an hour's worth of agenda

into a sixty-minute meeting, include about forty-five minutes' worth instead, and plan to end your meetings ten minutes early. Everyone will appreciate the unexpected extra time.

3 When meeting attendees have back-to-back meetings, especially on large company campuses, you'll either have to leave one early or arrive at one late. If you know this is true for one or more of your meeting attendees, speak with them to mitigate the problem ahead of time. While I'm on the topic of back-to-back meetings, scheduling your days like this really isn't efficient and can cause the time you spend in meetings to be wasted. You need time after every meeting to process thoughts, action items, notes, ideas, etc. This also goes for conference-type meetings, in which case you may have business cards, receipts, and other things to process. **So don't overschedule yourself.** A good rule of thumb is fifteen minutes of processing time for every hour of meeting you attend, which means you should schedule an hour of processing time for a half-day meeting and two hours of processing time after a day-long meeting. While it may not seem like you can spare the time, you'll get much more value out of the meetings you do attend when you build in processing time after. And if you find that occasionally you don't need the time, I'm sure you will find the unexpected unscheduled time to be a benefit!

4. Speak to those key people and get brief input ahead of time. That way, you might be able to keep the meeting on track with something like, "Kelly isn't here yet, but I know she is in general agreement on this topic, and here are the questions I know she has. Let's discuss them now so we'll be ready when she arrives." If the worst-case scenario is that the leader never makes it to the meeting, you may still be able to arm the leader with the ability to make a decision later.

5 If there are topics that don't require the latecomer's input, you can rearrange the agenda on the fly, but be careful of making this accommodation too often, because then people may take advantage and think they can be habitually late to your meetings. Also, you can invite people to show up to the meeting only for the agenda items that involve them.

6 If you are a leader and have a hard time getting to meetings on time, one reason might be because your meetings don't *end* on time. Another might be that your days are overscheduled. Both of these can be mitigated by ensuring your team is following the guidelines in this section. If you are insistent that meetings start and end on time, and that everyone is keeping a more realistic meeting schedule, you'll reduce the productivity drain that meetings are causing your organization.

DECIDE WHO SHOULD ATTEND

It's easy to send the meeting invitation to whomever crosses your mind, but that both makes your meeting less productive and takes valuable, productive time out of the days of your attendees.

Instead, take a little extra time to think about who you're inviting. Can each person on your list contribute something that advances the goals of the meeting? Are they the *best* people to make that particular contribution? Is there any redundancy on your list? Have you invited a whole team when you really just need one representative from that team present?

Be clear about the role of each person you're inviting, and share that role with them. Here are the typical roles of meeting attendees:

▸ **Decision-maker:** The decisions in this meeting will ultimately be up to this person.

▸ **Subject matter expert:** This meeting requires specific expertise that others in the meeting may not have.

▸ **Information sharer:** This person knows and will relay some history about your meeting's topic that will be useful during the discussion.

▸ **Timekeeper/scribe:** If the meeting organizer can't do this, invite someone who can keep the agenda on track and also capture the results of the meeting.

▸ **Information gatherer/representative:** This person represents a specific team or department and will be the one to speak for that team or department's interest in the meeting and report back to that team on the results of the meeting.

▸ **Bystander:** This is someone who is attending just for informational purposes, because they are interested or because it may be helpful to them, but they have no active role. They may be invited as a courtesy.

For the types of meetings you typically plan or attend, can you think of any other roles?

During the Meeting

Now that you've planned your meeting well, the next step is managing it effectively. Remember the advice in the "Honor the Clock" section, and encourage everyone to be empowered to keep the meeting on track with the timed agenda.

In addition, the way you close your meeting is critical. Every meeting should end with the following four questions (and make sure your scribe records the answers).

1. What decisions did we come to?

2. What *specifically* are the action items we decided were necessary?

3. Who *exactly* is responsible to complete these actions? (An individual person rather than a group, department, or team is best.)

4. When is the due date for these actions to be accomplished?

The first question is useful for clarity, ensuring everyone is in agreement. The second question helps to ensure that the meeting will advance an agenda. Without the third and fourth questions, the odds go down that the follow-up actions will actually get done within a timeline that is realistic for the responsible parties.

Another important consideration for a productive meeting is whether technology should be allowed. Here's a hint: the meeting will be more productive when it isn't. Ask everyone to leave their phones out of reach and take notes by handwriting them on paper or in a handwriting app in a tablet. These techniques are much less intrusive and distracting. They will also ensure that everyone is mentally as well as physically present so you can dispatch the agenda items as quickly and efficiently as possible.

After the Meeting

Use the information your scribe captured to create a summary of the meeting. Everyone who attended, plus any other stakeholders, should be sent a copy. Recipients are more likely to read (or at least skim) this summary if you put it in the body of the email instead of in an attachment.

The summary should include a recap of the answers to the four discussed earlier:

1   The decisions that were made in the meeting.

2   The action steps to be completed.

3   The people responsible for completing those actions (or the point person responsible for ensuring the actions get done).

4   The due dates for the actions.

Publicizing these commitments creates more accountability. If it's common in your organization to invite a lot of bystanders to meetings just to avoid hurt feelings or to keep everyone in the loop, mitigate this by emailing the meeting summary to all interested parties afterwards.

When You're Invited to a Meeting

Leaders can magnify their impact on the organization by following the meeting guidelines in this chapter.

Even if you're not a leader in your organization or the organizer of a meeting, you can still help make all the meetings you attend more productive.

REQUEST KEY INFORMATION

Before you decide to attend a meeting, ask the organizer three things if they aren't clear in the invitation:

1 What's the desired outcome of the meeting?

2 What's the agenda?

3 What role am I expected to play?

If the organizer can't answer those questions, that's a red flag that this meeting is going to be less productive than it should be, and that perhaps you shouldn't attend. Hopefully, your questions will encourage them to give the meeting some more thought!

If the organizer can provide the information you

requested, use it to determine whether you're the right person to attend the meeting. If you can't contribute to the goals of the meeting, or if it's not a priority for you when viewed in the context of your other work, opt out and tell the organizer who can contribute what they need. For example: "Oh, you invited me because you thought I went to that client meeting. Actually, I didn't. Kerrin went to that meeting. She'll offer more insight in the meeting than I can."

By doing this, you're putting more time back in your day, and you're helping the meeting be more productive for others.

PREPARE WELL

If you decide to attend the meeting, prepare well so you can make the contribution the organizer is expecting. Are you the decision-maker? An opinion giver? An information sharer? A subject matter expert? The role you are playing in the meeting dictates how you should prepare.

BE FULLY PRESENT

I know it's tempting to try to multitask during meetings. You might think you can still pay attention even while you're dashing off an email. But the best thing you can do for your own productivity and efficiency—and your team's—is to be fully present. By giving the meeting only part of your attention, you're less likely to offer useful input. If the meeting organizer doesn't insist on tech-free meetings, leave your devices out of reach anyway. The possible exception may be taking notes in a handwriting app on your tablet, but consider that having a tablet makes it tempting to click into other apps during the meeting. A better option may be to take notes by hand on paper and, at the end of the meeting, scan the notes into a scanner app on your phone and email the document to yourself for processing, either immediately after the meeting if you've scheduled the time according to the suggestion above, or later.

These strategies will help you plan productive

meetings and get more out of the meetings you are invited to attend. When you follow them, you'll accomplish more, and you'll help others accomplish more as well. You'll also be influencing the culture at your workplace. When you change your behavior around meetings, you influence others to take a look at their own habits.

CONCLUSION

No matter how you are communicating—email, text message, even in person—remember that you have a responsibility to convey information in a way that helps others be productive. That means remembering some courtesies like these:

▸ Consider *when* you are conveying information and whether it is the best time for your recipient. For example, don't relay detailed information that needs to be written down when you're talking to someone who's driving or who's rushing off to an appointment.

▸ We often choose the communication method that is easiest for *us* in the moment, instead of what would be most effective. Always think about whether you're using the best channel for what you're trying to accomplish. For example, if you're assigning someone a task that's due at a later date, don't use text messaging, which is more appropriate for shorter, more immediate communication. Instead, use email. That makes it easier for the recipient to assign the item to their task list.

▸ Don't hide behind your email or other technologies to distance yourself from a difficult situation. That only makes things worse.

▸ Be mindful of others' time when you communicate. For example, before posting a question to your office's chat platform, check whether the answer is already available on a previous thread or your company's intranet.

For more productive and efficient communication, don't treat information like a hot potato, believing that as long as you have tossed it to the recipient, you have fulfilled your obligation. When communication breaks down in an organization, it may not be because someone didn't **receive** information properly (for example, they missed an email or weren't listening in a meeting). Irresponsible **giving** of information due to one of the mistakes described earlier can also be a culprit.

Key Takeaways

▸ Email is real work that takes real time to complete.

▸ The TESST process can help you eliminate both digital and paper clutter by speeding your decision-making.

▸ Most people's workday plans are unrealistic, with

too many meetings, not enough time for email, and too little time to do thoughtful, proactive work.

- ▸ The way you communicate via email and other channels can enhance your productivity and support the productivity of others.

- ▸ Most workplaces have too many meetings that accomplish too little.

- ▸ Both organizers and attendees can make meetings more productive.

- ▸ Handling meetings more thoughtfully can give you—and others—more time for focused work.

Action Steps

▸ Set up some rules in your email, and visit *maura-thomas.com/tools* to select one or more email filtering apps or services.

▸ Estimate approximately how many messages you receive daily that fall into the "work" category as described earlier. Multiply that by two minutes per message, and leave the required amount of unscheduled time on your calendar to deal with this work.

▸ Start using the guidelines on writing productive emails (page 60) this week. Notice whether following these tips makes a difference in your productivity. For example, are you sending and receiving fewer emails? Are you experiencing fewer email miscommunications or inefficient back-and-forth exchanges?

▸ Take a look at any meetings on your calendar for which you are the organizer. Have you set a clear goal and agenda for each meeting and followed the other steps for efficient meetings? If not, start now!

▸ Now check your calendar for any meetings you are attending. Do you know the desired outcome, the agenda, and why you were asked to attend?

▸ If you are attending any meetings today, make it a point to be fully present. Don't check your email, glance at social media, or sneak in work on other tasks. Afterward, notice whether this helped you get more out of the meeting or make a more substantial contribution.

ACKNOWLEDGMENTS

Thank you for reading! My business, Regain Your Time, is the manifestation of my quest to provide busy, driven people with tools and strategies to regain control of their lives and work so that they can bring their unique gifts to the world in a way that makes them feel inspired and energized instead of stressed and overwhelmed. I'm excited for this Empowered Productivity Series to support that purpose.

You can find more information and ways to engage with me and Empowered Productivity at my website, maurathomas.com. It's full of resources to help you tackle individual and organizational productivity and live a happier, more productive, and more intentional life!

ACKNOWLEDGMENTS

This book would not be possible without the great team at Sourcebooks, and especially my dedicated and hardworking editor, Meg Gibbons. Thanks also to my agent, Rhea Lyons. Words can't express my gratitude for your efforts on my behalf. I also want to sincerely thank my team at Regain Your Time, including Shawn, Rita, Deena, Shana, Erin, Lisa, and Sam. I'm forever grateful for your dedicated support.

ABOUT THE AUTHOR

 **Maura Nevel Thomas** is an award-winning international speaker, trainer, and author on individual and corporate productivity and work–life balance, and she is the most widely cited authority on attention management.

She helps driven, motivated knowledge workers control their attention and regain control over the details of their life and work. Maura has trained over forty thousand individuals at over two thousand organizations on her proprietary Empowered Productivity System, a workflow management process for achieving significant results and living a life of choice.

Maura's clients include the likes of Dell, Old Navy, the U.S. Army, L'Oréal, the American Heart Association, NASA's Johnson Space Center, and Adobe. She is a TEDx speaker, successful entrepreneur, a Certified Speaking Professional from the National Speakers Association, and author of *Personal Productivity Secrets*, *Work Without Walls*, *Attention Management*, and *From To-Do to Done*. She is a media favorite, featured regularly in a variety of national business outlets, including the *Wall Street Journal*, NPR, *Fast Company*, *Entrepreneur*, *U.S. News & World Report*, and the *Huffington Post*. She is also a regular contributor to both *Forbes* and the *Harvard Business Review*, with articles there viewed over a million times.

Maura earned an MBA from the Isenberg School of Management at the University of Massachusetts and has studied the field of productivity all over the world for more than two decades.

Maura believes that every person has unique gifts to offer the world, and her purpose is to support them in offering those gifts in a way that is joyful and inspiring. She strives to have an impact that is relevant and unique, presenting new ideas and ways of thinking that are applicable to changing times.

Social impact is very important to Maura, so she is very active in her local community of Austin, Texas, where she has held volunteer leadership and mentor positions in a variety of different community organizations and charities. This belief also leads Maura to offer quarterly pro-bono presentations to nonprofits and to donate a percentage of all her business revenues to charity. Learn more at maurathomas.com.

NEW! Only from Simple Truths®

IGNITE READS
spark impact in just one hour

IGNITE READS IS A NEW SERIES OF 1-HOUR READS WRITTEN BY WORLD-RENOWNED EXPERTS!

These captivating books will help you become the best version of yourself, allowing for new opportunities in your personal and professional life. Accelerate your career and expand your knowledge with these powerful books written on today's hottest ideas.

TRENDING BUSINESS AND PERSONAL GROWTH TOPICS

 Read in an hour or less

 Leading experts and authors

 Bold design and captivating content